AF362562

Diary of a Stranger

Marika Strano

Diary of a Stranger © 2023 Marika Strano

All rights reserved.

No part of this publication may be reproduced, stored in a retrieval system, or transmitted, in any form or by any means, electronic, mechanical, photocopying, recording or otherwise, without the prior written permission of the presenters.

Marika Strano asserts the moral right to be identified as author of this work.

Presentation by *BookLeaf Publishing*

Web: www.bookleafpub.com

E-mail: info@bookleafpub.com

ISBN: 9789357440448

First edition 2023

To Marika.

*I know you're lost now, but I hope you have
a good map to come back home.*

I'm waiting for you.

May we meet again.

ACKNOWLEDGEMENT

Phaedrus wrote: "things are not always what they seem; the first appearance deceives many; the intelligence of few perceives what has been carefully hidden in the recesses of the mind."
There are not many people who know me well enough to try to decipher what has been carefully hidden in the recesses of my mind.

Among them there is my mom. My mind and soul have no secrets from her, I am like an open and vulnerable book, but when I am with her I don't feel in danger. Only in her arms I feel at home and safe. I wish I could live with her again. I hope on day it will happen.

I thank Diego, who in one of my moments of deep depression knew when to dial my phone number, even though I don't remember much of that call! He saved my life. He has brought a sort of relief to my soul since I have known him. I owe him at least a dinner, in his Tuscany of course! I hope we can come back to our favourite restaurant, Paolino, very soon.

I thank Eleonora, who always has many kind words in store for me. I am trying to learn to believe that I deserve them all. Eleonora, Emanuele and Chiara brighten my mornings with their messages, even though they are far away from me. I hope we can meet again in our Perugia, sooner or later.

As usual, then, I thank United Kingdom, and Wales in particular. It is giving me a great lesson in life and humility. And as I always say: "what doesn't kill you makes you stronger".

Finally, I thank those who have been with me during this terrible period, but my thoughts go to those who left me. This book (and more!) was born because of you moved away. I am grateful for this.

Marika

PREFACE

Between November 2022 and January 2023, I unfortunately started to suffer from depression. My days became longer and longer and more painful. Nothing and no one, except my mother's voice and my friends' phone calls, was enough for me to find a reason to live anymore. I cannot tell you more, here. This book is about love, and there is no space here for revenge or to regret some moments I lived or people that were part of my life. But let us remember that love is the noblest of feelings, but not when it destroys us instead of enriching us. Let us remember that we cannot love anyone else unless we first come to love ourselves.

When I decided to ask for help to my therapist, he asked me not only to write at least one page of diary a day, but also to try to write a poem, some verses that would allow us to identify that chaos of emotions I was feeling and to which I could not give a name. This is how Diary of a Stranger was born. I wanted to share my depression with readers, but in a way that could be useful to others to make them understand that, thanks to therapy and willpower, we can recover and reborn. I wanted also to reflect on the fact that too often we do not stop even one second to listen to our emotions. Our jobs, school and university are important, but we should also find time to breathe and try to understand how we feel, to name what we feel.

The book is divided into two parts: the first part is characterised by dark, gloomy verses and metaphors that recall the most terrible days, the days when I would just like to disappear or shut myself away in a silent nothingness. In the second part of the book, the verses are lighter and more colourful and represent the path taken, but not yet completed. They are an invitation not to give up, to learn more about one's limits and to try to go beyond them.

I hope that one day this pain, but also this incredible journey, may be of help not only to me, but also to many other people who for various reasons are going through (or have gone through) this experience of inner growth.

Marika Strano

Shards

In November, one night,
I cried.
On the floor, the shards
of a white and red cup
were stubbing my black soul.
Dark abyss.
My tears couldn't scratch them.
I pretended to hear his voice
from the other side of the reality.
He broke the silence,
preventing me from
listening to the chaos of
my chasm.
His words were such stuff
as the shards were made of.
Red shards.
Fire.
Red shards.
Blood.
A mirror looked at me:
Who are you?
I am a shard
made of fire and blood.

I was. I was not. Not anymore.

I looked for my reflection
in a corridor
of loneliness
and I saw my drunk shadow.
I was walking embracing
cold walls of ice,
echoes of my non-being.
Non-being anymore.
I was.
I was not.
Not anymore.
The old Enemy, lurking,
drew her weapons
against which
I hardly find forgiveness.
I, an obedient soldier,
was locked in two arms
clutching smoke.
With wide open eyes
I stared at his face.
His breathe on my neck,
chain of my soul.
I screamed hearing
The sweet whisper

of my Enemy's voice:
Run!
The chain wraps again
my naked body.
I was.
I was not.
Not anymore.

Kiss of a Jailer

Your
I love you
was the kiss
of a jailer.

Anxiety

When I stop in the middle of the street
I must remember to breathe.
I look at the sky, staring at his image
fixed in my mind and I ask myself
why.
My Enemy loves questions,
she cannot stand answers.
I live where I'm not and
I will never be.
Falseness turns into genuineness
and suddenly I can touch a nightmare.
Her weapons have killed many people
that I once knew
that I won't see again.
In my loneliness I tremble
like a leaf on burning ice.
Sometimes I pretend to be strong,
other times death seems
a wiser choice than life.
What's in a name?, The Poet wondered.
My name is Anxiety, the Enemy says.
In her name you can find
the story of my existence.
Why me? I ask.
She lurks, silent, in my heart,
while I stay gazing at the sky.

Night

Of that night
I only remember the coldness
of the moment you said
No, not anymore.
And I let you go.
Your embrace melted
like an ice cream in August
and the tight chains loosened
when I placed my hand on the screen
to say goodbye, amore.
I called your name
now meaningless
Because of that palpable lacerating pain.
I lost myself in you
and in you I will not find myself again.
What can I do now?
Thousand miles are waiting for me
to find my home again.
Where do I go
if my home was you?
Where am I now?
Of this night
I will only remember the coldness
when I whisper your name,
Lorenzo.

And one day,
when the warm torpor
will knock on my door,
I will mock these chains
that my mind has already loosened
and which my heart, instead,
tries to bind tighter.

To the Wind

I dedicated you
my words and my past,
many emotions and sacrifices.
You gave them
to the wind.

Christmas Eve's Dream

Warm and cozy lights.
A great celebration,
glittering decorations,
long, colourful dresses,
silk bow ties.
The chatter of people
who hadn't been seen for a year,
sparkling wine in red goblets
never empty.
Children running
looking for more chocolate.
My heart is in celebration
before the final act.
The curtain falls.

Sisyphus

Like Sisyphus
with a boulder
I climb mountains
of sufferings and pain.

As if Time

We live as if Time
belongs to us,
taking him for granted.
We forget he is
just a temporary gift that,
at a certain point of our journey,
is taken away from us
to be entrusted
to someone else.

Emptiness

I know you just want
to shout at the top of your voice
and instead you sigh
gazing in the
infinite emptiness.

Oxymoron

I am oxymoron,
nothing but oxymoron.
I seek the light
hiding in the dark,
freedom in lies.
I try to enrich myself
at the cost of my spirit.
We are oxymoron,
nothing but oxymoron.
Accepting this truth
Death, which is Life,
will cease to frighten us.
It will come to our banquet
with a white train
And we shall not be afraid
of the red wine
She will make us drink.

Post-it

An echo in you mind
screams you must move on,
while your soul is lost.
It is not written
on your post-it."
We all have a post-it
where fate has written
translatable words only if
we move the boulder forward.
Only if we decide to live
on day more.

7 a.m.

A coffee smells of productivity,
everything is still possible.
I sit in the garden
gazing a grey sunrise.
At 7 a.m. nothing and everything
has happened yet.
The excitement for a new day
is the sunlight
at the end of a grey tunnel.
Honest companion
who brings questions
worth trusting.

Pain's Kindness

The path to acceptance
is paved with Pain.
But if we stop thinking
we can start listen to
His noisy whispers and
words of kindness.
He's begging us to be kinder
with our feelings, to love
our storms and shards.

Love Declaration

I sit alone
at a coffee shop.
I am thinking that Love
has many faces and
when I see my reflection
in my coffee cup
I recognise that my smile
is the most beautiful
declaration of Love.

My Land

My Land is as complicated as I am.
the sun shines every day,
but Her past is wet with
an unceasing grey rain.
My bench waits for me
even when it knows
that the only place I can sit
is in my tired heart
that keeps looking at the sea.
the horizon becomes nostalgia,
the grains of sand tears.
I hear a friendly voice
but it is only the voice of the wind
that speaks another melodious language,
but not my own.
I sit on a bench
looking out over the ocean,
not my own,
which blends with
the blue of the sky
in summer and winter.
My sighs beg me
to come home,
to my bench,
not knowing, however, that

I am already here.
Not in the land where I was born,
but in the land where I will become.

Healing

Healing means loving ourselves
enough to accept that,
despite we are not invincibile,
we are worth of selflove
and respect.
Healing means being aware that,
even if there is obscurity inside of us,
we deserve to turn on our
spiritual light.
Healing means believing that
something better is around the corner
and that our inner peace is
right there for us.
We just have to trust
our timing.
We have to trust our inner voice
that knows we are worth only of
things that let us shine,
that let us live.

Pink Cloud od Candyfloss

How much time we lose
trying to control
something it is not in our power?
This is what takes away our freedom
to think the future,
to savour the present
for what it really is:
a moment already past,
a pink cloud of candyfloss
of which we still feel the taste,
but don't see the colour,
already made of dust.
The illusion of freedom
has vanished following
another future past yearning
which crumbles in our hands.
We should live our lives
like smiling children
on the merry-go-round
with their candyfloss
that tastes of"here and now".

Because they moved away or Gratitude

The beauty of travelling
with heavy luggage
is to understand
who will help me
to lift my thoughts and
the burdens of my life
when I look out the window
of the fast train that
is taking me nowhere
and everywhere.
When a shy ray of sunshine
will break through the clouds
my thoughts will fly over the track
of those who have gone away.
When my soul
will have breathed
a graceful sigh of relief,
I will show my gratitude,
thanking them.
It is thanks to them
if I am more confident,
if I have replaced
resentment with a smile,
hatred with a kind word.

I am stronger if I travel alone,
more stubborn if on the desk
of my crowded library
there is no one else but
my pride in my research.
And I will look back
just for a second:
I can exist again
because they moved away.

Diary of a Stranger

I get up every morning
In a bed of resentment
and repentance.
Where is my mother's hand?
The icy wind of my nothingness
has lost the cloud in which
I could feel her delicate touch.
My blankets are too thin
to cover me from my loneliness
and from the thoughts
that freeze my soul.
Then I remember that it is
early morning again,
that I can fill the pages
of this diary of a stranger
of words, oxygen for my torment.
When I get up,
I wipe away one tear
and I take the other with me
to remember that I can allow myself
to act like a human being
with my contradictions,
joys and light,
pain and darkness,
and that being a stranger

even to myself
in this gentle land
makes me what I was not,
but I am now,
And I accept it.

To myself

To the person who is
always there for me.
To the person who can support me,
whispering me kind words
on rainy days:
To myself.
To the person who dries my tears
and rejoices at my smile.
To the person I was ten years ago,
to the person I may become.
to the part of me that is lost,
to the part of me that I hope
to find again.
Remember to breathe
and to always try
to look forward even while
dancing in the rain.

www.ingramcontent.com/pod-product-compliance
Lightning Source LLC
LaVergne TN
LVHW051245200726
843510LV00011B/1694